Securing

Smiles

A Guide to Family

Security

By

Neil Huotari

ISBN: 978-0-615-33244-4

Illustrated by Aiden Huotari

Published by:
Aizax Security Solutions, LLC
P.O. Box 1300
Wayzata, MN 55391

Contents

Acknowledgements

I would like to thank my friends and colleagues who have encouraged me to write this book. Also, I would like to thank all the parents I spoke to, who shared their stories and questions on how to keep their family safe. In addition, I would like to thank Erin for editing this book and giving me a class in grammar 101. I hope I passed her junior high English class.

And above all, I want to thank my family. First my sons' Aiden and Zachary, who are high energy and live life to the fullest, they are extremely cool. Thanks for hanging out with dad this past summer. I also want to thank the General of our household, my wife Laurie. She has supported and encouraged me throughout my career and while writing this book. She edited and was my legal eagle while completing the book. She is a person I look up to and is my best friend. I could not have done this without her.

Thanks again for everybody who contributed and I hope that you will very much enjoy my book as well as find it incredibly educative!

Securing Smiles

Preface

Seeing a smile on a child's face is priceless. A child's smile represents the joy of learning from the world around them and the endless opportunities the future holds. I see a future of unlimited potential and many opportunities to spread their wings and change the world. In this fast paced and unpredictable world, protecting that smile is a responsibility that cannot be taken lightly. A parent, grandparent, Godparent, aunt or uncle, or any responsible child caregiver must understand the inherent risks that are present in our everyday routines. Being a parent of two high energy boys myself, I know and understand how busy these everyday routines can be. But I also know that parents will do anything for their children and make protecting them the highest priority in their life. I applaud parents and caregivers for their dedication and commitment in dealing with the daily grind that being responsible for a child demands and I offer this book to assist them.

At the beginning of the summer, my six-year-old asked me, "Daddy, how can I help you write your book?" I told him he could draw me a picture of our family and that would inspire me. Well, he drew me a picture alright and I was amazed how perfect that picture was. His picture grasped what a family security plan is all about. In his mind, a happy family is one that is holding hands smiling in front of a building. This building could be our house, hotel, a store or wherever we are together as a family. That is the true meaning and reason for a family security plan and that is why it is the front cover of my book. My son is now telling me when there is a car he doesn't recognize parked on our street and he also does not answer the door without Mom or

Dad with him. At his young age, he understands that having a basic security plan means our family will be happy and he knows he is a huge part of that plan. He understands his role.

Throughout my career, I have worked in many diverse and challenging environments. From 2000-2002 as a Military Police Officer, I was the commander of a 180 soldier Military Police Company. During that time, America was hit by the worst terrorist attack on American soil on September 11th, 2001. My Company was responsible for the physical security of a major airport in the Midwest and continued to prepare for follow up missions in support of Operation Iraqi Freedom. From 2002-2004, I was an anti-terrorism and urban combat instructor for the Army. I trained over 30,000 soldiers deploying to Iraq and Afghanistan.

In the Department of Justice, I spent ten years working for the Bureau of Prisons. I began as a correctional officer at the Federal Correctional Institution in Phoenix, AZ. Also, I was on a special operations response team that responded to emergencies within the prison such as riots, inmate cell extractions, drug raids, gang investigations and hostage rescue. My last position with the Bureau of Prisons was in inmate systems management, where I was responsible for processing inmates, transporting inmates and I was a Bureau of Prisons Hostage Negotiator.

In corporate America, I was a Security Intelligence Manager responsible for gathering and analyzing intelligence, identifying risks and implementing security measures to make people safer and teaching personal and international security to the employees.

My experience has given me a better understanding of the risks that are faced by individual's every day. I know how important it is to teach people the basics about security. I want to use what I have learned to help families build a stronger family security plan to fit their busy life-styles. I want to assist in keeping families safe.

In this book, I use scenarios (based on real life incidences) to describe everyday threats and to identify proactive steps for families that will mitigate the risk of violence and crime against family members. I firmly believe if you are aware of your surroundings and follow basic principles and methods, you can deter criminals from invading your personal life.

I want all parents to think proactively about their family security and to be aware of things that just don't look right. I want parents to teach their children how to be aware of their sur-roundings and what to look out for. Because at the end of the day when you have time to reflect about life, each one of us understands that our highest priority is to our children and our most important mission is "Securing Smiles."

Securing Smiles

Chapter 1: Security Is Personal

As a nine year old boy, I road my bike around town without my parents worrying or many times not even knowing where I was. Their biggest worry was whether I got hurt making crazy jumps with my Huffy bike or playing football with the Mattison boys. They never would have imagined that someone would be out to hurt their child.

We kept our house doors unlocked day and night and kept the car unlocked with keys in the ignition and windows open. Crime was low. People did not worry about crime because you did not hear about anybody you knew becoming victims. Times have changed and now we are in a totally different society. This forces us to be aware of what our family members and our loved ones are doing and to have some sort of a plan to ensure their safety.

People now have to lock their doors and pay attention to what their kids are doing and where they are. We are living during a time in which there are people who will do harm to your family or you. I am not saying that there weren't these types of people walking the streets in the 70's and 80's. There were. But you did not hear about as many incidents as we are hearing about now. This may be because the media has a tendency to report crime as headlining stories, while the heroic story gets moved down in the broadcast or doesn't make the front page. It may also be because, for some reason, the negative stories seem to be easier to remember than the positive stories. Now is a time when, as parents, we need to take a look at our surroundings and ensure we have an understanding of the risks that our children and family are experiencing each day.

A piece of good news reported on July

24th, 2009, was a headline in the Minneapolis Star Tribune that read, "Drop in crime is a victory." In Minneapolis and other major U.S. cities, there has been a drop in violent crimes. According to the Minneapolis Police Department statistics, overall, violent crime dropped more than 25 percent since 2007 and nearly 18 percent in the past year alone. Even property crimes have fallen 11 percent in the first half of 2009 compared with the same period last year, and have dropped 23 percent since 2007. Minneapolis city leaders credited smart policing, efforts to curb juvenile violence and targeting the most violent offenders for big drop in violent crime.

But police departments need our help. Citizens play a major role in the fight against crime by communicating to the police suspicious behaviors and potential criminal acts. How many times have you seen police talk to citizens on the street, talk to employees at a store or talk to fans at a ballgame? They do this because these are places where information is shared and relationships are made.

It is our responsibility to introduce our children to what is safe in this world and what is not. Every time my sons see a police officer they smile and know that they are there to protect them. I have explained to them that a police officer's job is to keep us safe.

This past summer, I had the unique opportunity to take the summer off and spend it with my two boys. We did many things I have never done before and visited places I have never have gotten to experience as a Dad. We went to many public parks, lakes, malls, walks and also visited local libraries. We had a blast. It was also a time where I had a chance to sit back and partake in a hobby called "people watching." During this time, I had a chance to interact with parents who were watching their children. When I shared with them my past security career, the conversation usually went to them telling me about observations they have made about security and asking my opinion on what they should or could have done regarding various situations. They wanted to know more about what to look for and who to look for. A common sentiment among parents is they want to be prepared for the risks their children face with and without them around.

Speaking with the parents reemphasized one thing: parenting or watching a child is not easy. I will use a statement that my wife often says to me, "Your boys are not your little soldiers!" Yeah, that is definitely true. After spending ten years with the Department of Justice and fifteen years in the US Army, I know one thing. Being a dad is the toughest and most challenging assignment by far. It is also DEFINITELY the most rewarding. Children are the reason we work so hard and strive to make a safe and loving world for them. We would do anything for our children because we are their protector and are committed to keeping them safe.

Securing Smiles

Chapter 2: Be Aware

It was a beautiful sunny morning and I had just finished all my training as a Correctional Officer for the Bureau of Prisons. I was set to embark on my first solo as the officer in charge of the education center containing 400 inmates. I walked through the front gate of the prison and received my keys, radio and body alarm, and proceeded to the education center. I was extremely confident that I could handle whatever the inmates would throw at me. I THOUGHT I was a tough guy (who grew up on the tough streets of a town of 287 people in northwestern Minnesota). Well, I was in for a lesson that changed my opinion about the meaning of toughness.

As I was walking through the education center's main hallway, I heard a lot of loud talking coming from the big classroom at the end of the hall. I stuck my chest out, chose not to call for backup and ran to the classroom. As I opened the door, my adrenaline was pumping hard and I was excited to tell the inmates who I was and that I was intent on squashing their illegal assembly.

As I threw open the door and dashed to the middle of the room, I abruptly halted my mission and sheepishly looked at about 75 inmates who were part of one of the largest most organized gangs in the prison. I instantly transformed from a cocky twenty-three–year-old, to a two-year-old wanting my teddy bear and blanket. I had just interrupted a major organized prison gang meeting! In their minds, I possibly heard something they did not want staff to hear. So, as I stood in their midst feeling like the honorary pig waiting to be the main course for the upcoming luau, I awkwardly apologized for the interruption and hustled out of the room. To my surprise, nobody stopped me. I went straight to the Lieutenant's office and told him about our problem. A couple months later, that same gang rioted in our prison which caused damage to buildings and property and injured many people.

Identifying Risks:

I realize that the example above is not a situation that most of you will encounter. I share this with you as an example of how being aware of your surroundings is important. You should always be aware. Be aware of your surroundings and take notice of things that appear to be out of the ordinary.

If you think before you act, there is a greater possibility that you will avoid dangerous events or at least have time to react when they occur. In the scenario above, I learned a valuable lesson about awareness that has stuck with me for seventeen years. I make it a point to understand and be proactive when identifying threats. For example, when I walk into a restaurant or store, I identify where all the exits are. I also look for people acting strangely or things that seem out of the ordinary. I want to know what I am walking into so I can make a conscious decision about how I will act if something were to occur.

Regarding my prison experience above, I am acutely aware that my situation could have had a far worse outcome. I have learned the importance of identifying the types of behaviors and actions that may lead to an unsafe area or condition. I believe in keeping my eyes open and staying in tune to the world around me and who's around my family.

That said, we have to find a balance between awareness and fear. We cannot let anxiety and apprehension control our lives. It is important to be honest with your child about community dangers, while avoiding the introduction of unnecessary stress into your child's life. This balance is important. You are the best judge of your child's character and you know the best way to communicate this message to him or her. It may help to explain that the situations being discussed do not happen often, but are still important to be prepared for, just in case.

It is natural to feel threatened, especially when the headlines are continuously talking about thefts, carjacking, rapes and murders. A little healthy concern can motivate us to live smart. We need to think about where we are traveling and take proactive security steps to be ready if something happens. If a place appears to be a risk, change your plans. We need to take control by being the decision maker, rather than having to react to a situation that surprises us.

I think we all agree that if confronted by a person who demands your wallet and money, it is best to give it to him or her. Your possessions are just material things. If the person tries to take you by force, try everything you can to get away. The more you fight, the less that person will be inclined to take you because a criminal does not want to get noticed and he or she certainly does not want to get caught. Tell your kids that if someone tries to grab them, or a stranger should approach them, they should run away, scream as loud as they can and find their Mom, Dad or a trusted adult. They should use statements like, 'Stranger!' 'You are not my Mommy or Daddy!' 'Help!' 'Fire!' or 'Call 911!' Make as much noise as you can, scream, scream and scream!

Because many of our everyday activities are automatic, we hardly think anything bad can happen. And nine times out of ten it probably won't. But are you willing to take that chance? Is the man who has been following you for three blocks going to the same place you are, or is that just a coincidence? Is the adult stranger watching your child at the park with extreme interest just a nice guy who likes kids, or is he having negative thoughts? What if you came out of the store one night and you saw a creepy man standing by your car on his cell phone? Is he really talking to somebody? Where do you go? Who can you call? Your children need your direction.

The direction you give your child can depend on your individual awareness to the world around you. If you are not taking security seriously, your child won't. Making your children more aware will allow them to be more observant of the world around them and make better and safer decisions. This starts with you leading by example. A parent must limit all modern day distractions (i.e. use of cell phones, PDAs/Smartphone's and headphones) and know what is going on in the immediate area of their child. Controlling your environment is much easier when your children are with you. The true challenge starts when your children are old enough to venture off with other people. Your research and lessons do not stop once they leave your home, but will continue on through adulthood. This is why a solid foundation about security at a young age is extremely important.

I often here parents say, "I don't want to shelter my children too much because I want them to be ready to handle all that life has to offer, both good and bad." I totally agree that children need to learn what is right and wrong, but we need to instill proactive planning and common sense security measures that can make their learning experience safer and lessen the everyday threats that they will be facing. Help your children to learn how to observe and how to tell when something doesn't look right. Furthermore, tell them where to go and who to tell when they see something that doesn't look right. As any law enforcement officer will tell you, complacency is a problem. People get comfortable with their surroundings and let their guard down. They may think that bad things only happen to other people and do not occur in their neighborhood. I am here to tell you that you are taking an unnecessary risk by thinking this way. I do not want you to become paranoid, just in tune to what is going on. We must stay alert in our surroundings on the street, in an office building, at a shopping mall, while driving, or waiting for a bus or cab. Know the neighborhood you live in. Know and observe when something does not look right. If you are unsure, call the police.

If you choose to do an activity such as running, walking, biking, skate boarding, rollerblading, or any outdoor activity, you should not wear any type of ear phones. You need to be aware of what is going on in the world around you. Each day, I see teenagers wearing their headphones outdoors and not paying attention. Just the other day, my wife and I were driving on a busy road and a teenager was riding his bike while wearing his headphones. He crossed a heavily traveled street and nearly ran right into the side of our car. He would have if I had not been paying attention. He did not know I was there because he was too into his music. So keep the headphones off and listen to what is going on around you.

Tips:
- Teach your children that a stranger is ANYONE they don't know.
- Instruct your children to know that it is okay to say NO to an adult if they feel uncomfortable, even if it seems rude.
- Check your neighborhood to see if there are

any known sex offenders in your area by using the National/State Sex Offender Website which is coordinated by the Department of Justice and located at: http://www.fbi.gov/hq/cid/cac/registry.htm

- Use safety drills, similar to what kids regularly do at school, to point out the importance of being observant and to see if your kids understand what you expect.

- You need to teach your children that NO ONE has the right to touch them if they don't want them too.

- Teach your children that it is right to tell mommy or daddy if an adult asks them to keep a secret or says, "It's our little secret."

- Instruct your child that he or she should never get into anyone's car without your permission.

- Teach them to never take candy or gifts from a stranger.

- Ensure your children understand that he or she should not help an adult stranger.

- Teach your child to scream and run away if a strange car pulls up beside them or if someone tries to force them into a car or building.

- As a parent, you need to limit your children wearing clothing or carrying items with their name printed on the outside. If they do, make sure they understand if a stranger says their name, it is not because they know them, but because it is written on their shirt.

- Teach your children to never say they are alone when they answer the phone and should never answer the door if they are alone.

- Remind your child to not invite people into

your home without your permission.

- Communicate to your children the importance of them letting you know where they are at all times.

- Teach your children that playing in deserted buildings and isolated areas is dangerous and they should not do it.

- Teach your children how to identify safe people (like store clerks, mothers with children, and police officers) if ever lost.

- Talk with your children about the importance of police officers. Your children need to know that police officers can help them, if needed.

- Never leave your child unattended, even for a minute.

Parent's Checklist:

- I have a recent photo of my child, his/her fingerprints, and a current record of his/her height and weight.

- I never mark my child's clothing or toys with his/her name, but rather I use my child's or my own initials instead.

- I make a mental note of what my child is wearing every day.

- I carefully check babysitter and child care references.

- I know my child's friends' names, addresses and phone numbers.

- I always accompany my young child to a public bathroom.

- If my child is old enough to stay alone, I designated a neighbor's home as a "safe house" where my child can go if I'm not home and there is an emergency.

- I always know where my child is.

Chapter 3: Teach Your Children About Security.

Police are investigating after a woman allegedly attempted to lure a ten-year-old boy into her car near a local high school. According to the police, the woman tried to get the boy to come with her by telling him that his mother was in the hospital. She also offered to give him pizza. The boy, who was attending baseball practice on a field near the school, refused to go with her even after she told two baseball coaches the same story. She left the scene without further incident. The boy's parents arrived shortly thereafter and said the woman was lying.

Identifying Risks:

As a child growing up in the 70's and 80's, I was taught to respect all adults. Saying no to an adult was never discussed and was usually frowned upon. In the above scenario, a woman created a story to try and lure a ten-year-old boy to go with her. He did not believe her and said no. The boy was likely coached by his parents to know that they would never send a stranger to pick him up. In today's world, a child needs to know that it is okay to say no when an adult crosses the line. Teaching children the skill of saying no must begin at an early age. As children get older, we also need to teach them how to assess a potentially dangerous situation and how to recognize it. This is very important, especially for teenagers. Make sure you communicate with your child in a manner that he or she will understand at their age and maturity level. You want your message of safety to be heard, understood and practiced by your child.

I believe it is imperative that parents take the time to understand and recognize the possible

19

risks facing their children. When I take my boys to a store, it is a rule that they are always by me. Last winter, we were at the grocery store and my three-year-old decided it would be a good idea to run and play hide and seek with Daddy. We were in the pasta isle. He looked at me with a huge mischievous smile and took off running. I told him to come back, but as each parent has probably experienced, that just made him run faster in the other direction. My five-year-old knew what his brother did was wrong and stayed right by my hip. I ran after my three-year-old and found him hiding under the grapes in the fruit section. He looked at me with his big blue eyes and said, "Are you happy with me, Daddy?" Right there, knowing I had to be stern and not give in to his cute face, I said, "You don't run away from me! You scared Daddy and I love you very much." He knew he was wrong and he apologized by saying, "I'm *vewy, vewy sowwy* Daddy." I have tried to instill in both my children that they must communicate with me before they go anywhere. And if they forget, I remind them and they know it. And they do forget because, remember, they are children. That is why being consistent in teaching is a must for parents, especially in an uncontrolled environment with smaller children. Children have to know and understand how serious you are about their safety.

Twenty years ago, parents did not think their child could be abducted while walking to school, assaulted while going to the grocery store or snatched at the county fair. Now, because of incidents involving crimes against children, this is a harsh reality of the world we live in. In today's society, one must pay more attention to what our children are doing and where they are going and with whom they interact. We must be tuned into the world around us and around them.

We must take notice of that suspicious car in the neighborhood or that suspicious man walking in the neighborhood. As we look at a newspaper, internet website, or the television, the glaring headlines are telling us that crime is happening and it is affecting the average American.

Parents must teach children from an early age about boundaries. These are your parental rules regarding such things as who they can see or visit and what they can do, how they will get there and where they may go. The rules should consider how long they may be away and how they get in contact with you if plans change. Your boundaries may also consider and encourage the importance of family time, open communication as well as internet and mobile phone usage.

Just as important, is to teach our children to recognize inappropriate behaviors. A stranger giving them candy, offering a ride, or requesting to take a picture, are examples of triggers. These are instances in which the child needs to get out of the area and run to a safe place to tell an adult so the bad person will get caught.

Discussing these situations as a family helps children recognize potential danger. Explain to a child that if a person makes you feel scared or uneasy, even if you know them, that is not the way adults should act. Instruct the child that if someone acts strange or gives you an uncomfortable feeling, get out of the situation and go to the adult caring for you. Most cases of abuse and abduction happen with peers or adults that your child knows. Children have the right to say no.

As I said in the beginning, saying no is a good thing. If someone does something your child does not like, tell your child that it is all right to use his or her voice to assert power. Have your children also practice saying no. Tell them to whisper no, scream no and yell no. Teach them to say no like they mean it until they are confident saying it. Repeat it. Communicate to your children that saying no is not a bad thing and ensure they understand the importance. It is their right to say NO and it must be respected by the recipient. Their voice gives them options of screaming for help and telling the world that something is not right. If a child is silent, they may not be heard when needed.

Try to keep an open family communication style so that issues affecting your child can be discussed. You are far more likely to have your child tell you their fears and concerns if you are open and willing to listen. Don't judge what they say and don't finish their sentences for them. If it takes them a while to explain, give them the time.

Finally, it is extremely important that one parent knows where their children are at all times. When young children are outside, place them in the specific care of a trustworthy person, and do not leave them unattended or alone. Instruct children to keep doors and windows locked, not to admit strangers, and to call their parents if there is a knock on the door. If possible, place your child's room in a part of the home not easily accessible from outside, and lock any doors providing access to it from the outside, especially in the evening. Keep interior doors to a child's room open to be able to hear any unusual noises. Set aside family time to talk about security as your children grow up. And above all, let them make some decisions. You know and love your child more than anyone, so make sure you teach them about security to keep them safe.

Tips:

- Teach your children to not answer the door when they are home alone and to not tell callers when they are home alone.

- Teach your children not to talk to strangers or offer personal information to anyone they do not know.

- Explain to your child that just because someone knows their name, it does not mean he or she needs to go to them or talk to them. This is especially true if they are wearing a shirt with their name on the back like a sports uniform. Be cognizant of what they are wearing.

- Teach your children that no one has the right to touch them or ask them personal questions.

- Teach your children to not hitchhike or accept rides from strangers.

- Teach your children or teen to be honest with you about where they have been and who they have seen.

- Teach your children to tell you where they are going and when they will be back. Make sure they know all your phone numbers including work and cell phone numbers, or write these numbers on a card and they can carry it with them so they can always reach you.

- Know where your children are playing. Have them stay away from empty buildings, alleys, and other places that might be dangerous. Emphasize that they are always safer in a group.

- Explain to your children that if they see something that doesn't seem right, like an unrecognized car driving around the block again and again, they should tell an adult right away. This will assist in keeping your neighborhood safe.

- Discuss the rules about strangers with your children. Tell them don't talk to them, don't go anywhere with them, and don't take anything from them. If ANYTHING makes your child feel uncomfortable, he or she should get away and go to your safe house or home.

- Have a family secret code word that only the family knows. This code must be used to identify the safe person if a child is to be picked up in an emergency situation by someone other than his or her parent or known adult or trusted caregiver.

Five Do's for parents to keep talking with their child:

- Listen carefully. Everyone, especially teenagers, likes to feel heard. When adolescents voice their opinions and views of the world, take time to listen respectfully to what they're saying.

- Don't jump to conclusions. Sometimes kids, especially teens, can take a long time to get to the point of a story. Try not to respond until you actually hear the end of a story.

- Praise kids when they ask for help. For example say, "I'm really glad you told me that, I appreciate your honesty."

- Respect their worries and concerns, even if they're different from your own.

- Remind your teens periodically that they should come to you if someone is threatening them or intimidating them at school, or anywhere else.

Chapter 4: Keeping Your Home Secure

Like a lot of people who use social media, a family recently went on Twitter to share real-time details of a recent trip. Their posts said they were "preparing to head out of town," that they had another 10 hours of driving ahead," and that they "made it to Kansas City."

While they were on the road, their home was burglarized. The father owned an online video business with 2,000 followers on Twitter. A detective from the local police department, which is investigating the burglary said: "You've got to be careful about what you are putting on the social media. You never know who's reading it."

Identifying Risks:

According to the Department of Justice statistics, approximately 1.4 million homes are burglarized in the United States each year. Most home burglaries occur during the month of August, when homeowners are away traveling on vacation. As in the above example, when you leave your house, make sure you not only secure your house, but only tell a trusted few that you are gone. The above family thought by sharing their vacation on twitter, they would be sharing their vacation with their all their friends and family. But what actually happened was that a burglar used a computer to log onto the father's Twitter web site and knew the family was away from their house. He then proceeded to rob their house.

This was not a random act. It could have been prevented. It was a planned operation. The burglar saw this house as an easy target. The burglar knew this family was gone by their use of Twitter to broadcast their journey. Do not make your home vulnerable when you are away.

Securing Smiles

A belief that your home is a safe haven should be a paramount goal for all families, whether you live in a house or an apartment. Knowing your home is safe provides peace of mind both when you are away and when you are home.

The first step in making your home secure is to evaluate your current security measures. Contact your local police department to determine if they will provide a free security inspection of your home. You can also ask your family and friends to pretend to be burglars and make their best attempts at entering your home. Just make sure they let you know before they do it. The objective of this exercise is to identify every vulnerable area of your home. If it is not difficult to find the key hidden under the flower pot, a burglar could locate it, too. Can you climb your oak tree and gain access to a second floor window? A limber thief could do the same.

Darkness and shadows offer additional opportunities for burglars, so perform this exercise at night as well. Does your landscaping cover or cast a shadow on doors and windows? It could also conceal a thief at work. You also do not want to encourage burglars by making it obvious that you have valuables inside your residence. After your inspection, make a list of all potential trouble spots. Fortunately, there are simple inexpensive solutions to most of your problems. Such as, motion sensing lights, dead bolts for all doors, leaving your yard lit if away or at night or putting up a security sign in a visible place in front of house.

When people think of protecting their homes, they often think of fancy expensive security systems with lots of bells and whistles. That is certainly an option, but there are measures you can take that are inexpensive, or even free. Also, depending on your home and neighborhood, you may not need the most expensive system on the market. In fact, no single device, including a home security system, will make your residence completely safe. You do not want a thief to get close enough to your home to determine if you have a burglar alarm. The most effective home security program is one that deters burglars as soon as they view your residence.

There are also other actions you can perform while you are at home which will make your home safer. They are simple common sense security measures I call home security family actions. When you are out in the backyard mowing or working on the landscape, have your garage door closed. If you have a door to your house located in your garage, a burglar will gain access to your house if you leave your garage open. Also, keep your valuables (i.e. wallets, purses, keys) located out of sight. Do not leave them lying on the counter of the kitchen or in kitchen drawers or in a cabinet located by the entrance of your house. Find a place that is not by a regular walkway in your house.

Do not leave toys, tools or lawnmowers outside in your yard. Make sure they are put away in your garage or shed. If you leave them out, this gives off a message that you are not paying attention to your property and could be viewed as a weakness by a burglar driving by.

Finally, be alert when someone is walking or driving in your neighborhood who you do not recognize. Acknowledge that person so he or she knows you are paying attention. Being attentive and alert when you are in your yard is good because it makes a statement that says you care about who comes into your neighborhood. Seeing a homeowner aware of their surroundings will hopefully make a potential burglar look at other targets.

Tips:

Walk around your house and ask yourself, "If I was a burglar and going to break in to my house, where would be my most likely place to do it?" This will give you an awareness of points of entry that are attractive to someone wanting to get into your house. Below are some things you might see:

If there is a dark area, install a motion detector light. Most criminals are attracted to targeting easier areas with poor lighting. Placing motion detector lights around your property can help you in a few ways. First, they can be set to turn on any time someone (including you) approaches the property. This works great for areas such as the front door or walkways. When you walk to the door, the lights will turn on. You won't need to fumble in the dark for keys or keyholes, and visitors have their way lighted without stumbling through the dark. The lights then turn themselves off and will turn back on automatically when needed. Most security lighting is pretty basic to install.

If there are large or overgrown shrubs around the house, trim the shrubs, especially if they are located by a window or next to a door because they provide good places for thieves to hide. If shrubs are desired at these locations, select ones with thorns to deter potential intruders. Thorny plants can also be used near adjacent trees or other structures so intruders will be less likely to climb and attain access to upper levels. Examples of thorny shrubs include barberry, hawthorn, holly, fire thorn, bramble, currant and rose shrubs. Pick one that is right for the landscaping of the property as well as the security of the home. In addition, cut back any tree branches that hang over the home roof and remove lower limbs from any trees next to the home. This will prevent a burglar from climbing to gain access to the second floor.

Look close at the front door or other doors accessible to your home. If the door is made out of a flimsy composite or could be destroyed by a kick, then replace it. For a door to be considered well secured, it must be constructed from either metal or solid hardwood. Plywood, USB or MDF wood composites usually have a weaker material structure. They do not possess the elastic qualities of solid hardwood or metal and tend to fail more easily once under pressure or strain.

Regarding glass sliding doors, a burglar can break through the glass or pry the door off the track to open it. Consider enhancing your security measures a bit. There are many expensive devices you can use other types of inexpensive devices. As you see in many homes, people use a broom handle on the inside track of the sliding door so it cannot be forced open. You can also purchase a long bar called a Charlie bar which are recommended by many law enforcement agencies. Although this bar might be unsightly, use it during the night or when you are away from home.

Additional tips:

- All entrances, including service doors and gates, should have quality locks, preferably deadbolts.

- Do not keep your home address in your car.

- Don't give specific information about your schedule on your outgoing voicemail or on automated 'out-of-office' email replies. Offer a cell or alternate number on your message.

- Don't leave keys hidden outside the home. Rather leave an extra key with a trusted neighbor or colleague.

- Keep doors locked even when family members or you are at home.

- Have window locks installed on all windows. Use them.

- Have locks installed on your fuse boxes and external power sources.

- If you have window grilles and bars, review fire safety. Don't block bedroom windows with permanent grilles if the windows may be used for emergency egress.

- Keep at least one fire extinguisher on each floor, and be sure to keep one in the kitchen.

- Periodically check smoke detectors and carbon monoxide detectors and replace batteries when necessary.

- Keep flashlights in several areas in the house. Check the batteries often, especially if you have children in your home.

- A family dog can be a deterrent to criminals. But remember, even the best watch-dog can be controlled by food or poison. Do not install separate "doggy doors" or entrances.

- Choose a home that offers the most security. The less remote, the safer your home will be, choose a neighborhood close to police and fire protection.

- Know your neighbors. Develop a rapport with them and offer to keep an eye on each other's homes, especially during trips.

- Never chat with a stranger about leaving your

home for a vacation. You never know who may be watching for an opportunity for a break-in.

- Establish safe family living patterns. If you understand the importance of your contribution to the family's overall security, the entire household will be safer.

- While at home, your family and you should rehearse safety drills and be aware of procedures to escape danger and get help.

- Vary daily routines and avoid predictable patterns.

- Know where all family members are at all times.

Tips for picking out a home alarm system:

- The average cost of a burglar alarm is $2,300.00. (U.S. Department of Justice Statistics)

- Make sure the installer describes to you how an emergency call works. Have him or her explain their 24/7 central monitoring system so you are confident help will be there in your time of need.

- In most areas of the country, you will have a choice of several well-known home alarm system providers which work with local installers and offer alarm systems at a discount or even free if you purchase a monthly monitoring service through them.

- When working with an installer, make sure you thoroughly understand where they intend to locate the control panel and how they expect each sensor to communicate with the alarm/ control panel. (Usually they are by the front/back doors and master bedroom.)

- Sensors are usually grouped into zones and zones communicate back to the alarm panel. Again, make sure you understand how each zone is going to interact with the control panel.

- Make sure the home alarm system you're choosing has all of the features you're interested in such as burglar, carbon monoxide, smoke, heat, temperature and water sensors.

- Have the installer demonstrate to you how the key pad and control panel work before deciding on an alarm system. Make sure the codes and the overall security process does not seem overly complex to you. Make sure you understand how to arm and disarm the alarm before they leave.

- If you have a pet, make sure the motion detectors are set to the pet's size so they will not cause false alarms once the motion detectors have been activated.

Chapter 5: Who Are You Letting Into Your Home?

ABC News 20/20 reported that a major appliance service company settled a lawsuit for an undisclosed amount with a woman who was assaulted in her home by one of its carpet cleaners. The worker had a long criminal record when he started cleaning carpets for the company. Though he technically worked for a subcontractor that did not do a background check, the victim filed a lawsuit against the appliance service company. The company now requires background checks of all their home service workers.

Identifying Risks:

Many law enforcement officials believe all employers who provide home services should conduct background checks and they should not hire anyone with a criminal record.

Background checks are a must for anyone you have watch your children or perform work in your house or on your property. If you are hiring a landscape crew or a roofing crew, make sure they have completed background checks on each employee that works on your property. A reputable contractor will have background checks completed and documented and will show you upon request.

If you have solicitors come to your house, I strongly encourage residents to take appropriate precautions when answering the door. First, make sure the solicitor is employed by the company they claim to represent. Check out their credentials (many wear an identification badge around their neck or they will have it in their hand) before you open the front door. Before you pay money to anyone selling goods or services door-to-door, or allow any salesperson into your home, understand the credentials they need in order to conduct business in your city. Requirements vary so check with your local city clerk's office. Do not hesitate to call 911 if an unlicensed solicitor approaches your home or you. The police department can send a patrol officer to your area to contact the unlicensed solicitor. REMEMBER YOU DON'T HAVE TO OPEN THE DOOR!

The safety of you and your family is of the utmost importance. Remember, when you open that door, you are exposing your family to a possible unknown threat or risk. So be cautious and aware before you open the door.

Tips:
Dealing with door-to-door salespeople:

- Ask to see a solicitor's license or credentials before listening to a sales pitch. Get the address and phone number of the company the solicitor works for. If the person does not represent a known business, ask for references and check them out before making a purchase.

- Take time to think it over. A reputable salesperson will agree to come back the next day or the next week. Allow yourself time to compare deals.

- Be careful with how much information you divulge about yourself to a solicitor during a conversation.

- Do not allow any solicitor to come inside your home for any reason. Allowing strangers inside your home can compromise your personal safety or allow them an opportunity to view valuables in your home. Talk outside or through a security screen door. If you want the salesperson to come back for a more extensive presentation, ask a friend or family member to be with you in your home.

- Remember that you have the right to ask a salesperson to leave at any time. If they will not leave when asked, call 911.

- Be wary of solicitors who are overly aggressive, persistent, intimidating or threatening.

- Do not be afraid to say no.

Hiring a Nanny

A nanny allegedly stole checks from the homes of her employers. She moved from job to job and committed a crime at each stop. She even showed up at a local day care to pick up a child after having been let go by the child's parent's months before. After the day care incident, police found the woman working as a nanny for another family and arrested her. According to police, the woman came to America on a work permit. She did so well on her interviews at the homes where she worked as a live-in nanny that most families never checked her references or ran a background check. This is how she managed to steal sensitive financial information from the people for whom she worked. In one instance, police said the nanny cashed forged checks totaling $21,000.

This nanny is a prime example of why people need to protect themselves when hiring an in-house employee, particularly one in charge of watching children like a nanny, babysitter or an au pair. When people allow someone into their house, they should know that person's background.

The interview process is a two step process. First, you should conduct an interview. Do not get caught up on an incredible interview and hire the individual prematurely. Anybody can give a strong interview, especially deceptive people. The interview process should include filling out an application form detailing his or her work history including references should be checked to ensure they are legitimate. If the references check out, the next step is to conduct a background check. Background checks should also be performed by a professional, accredited background check provider to ensure maximum efficiency. Make it a priority to know more about the person watching your children than that person knows about you!

Steps for hiring a nanny:
1. **Define expectations of nanny:** Make sure the person you are hiring is a fit for your family environment and your children's personality.
2. **Determine your level of trust:** Reputable nanny agencies that do pre-employment screening are expected to have more reliable nannies than private individuals posting their ads in the local newspaper. Get references from your close circle of family or friends, trusted neighbors or fellow church goers. However, just because the applicant was referred by a friend or a nanny agency, does not mean she or he should receive less scrutiny during the interview process.
3. **Conduct an initial interview:** The first impression is important, but it can also be very misleading. Remember, the candidate may know the right words to say to make you think they are right for the job; however the candidate's dependability and strengths should not be determined from an initial interview. If the candidate passes the initial interview, then proceed and check the references. Do not conduct initial interview with your kids

present.

4. **Use an employment application:** Use an application to obtain the necessary information including the candidate's name, date of birth, social security number, driver's license number. If the applicant refuses to cooperate with the application or background check process, do not hire him or her.

5. **Call references:** If references are good, proceed to background check.

6. **Nanny's background:** Very important. There are many strong in depth background verification companies that can help. If using a nanny service ask what background check company they are using. Check the State Attorney General's or Secretary of State's office to ensure the background check company you choose is a legitimate company.

7. **Conduct a second interview:** If the background check is passed and the applicant has a clean criminal record, proceed with the second interview. Have your children present to watch the potential employee interact with them.

Securing Smiles

Chapter 6: Neighbors Are An Important Ally For Your Home Security

In November 2007, 2 persons were involved in an armed robbery at a store in Milwaukee, Wisconsin. They fled the scene prior to the arrival of police. Based on observations reported to the police by one of its citizens, information was passed on to other area law enforcement agencies leading to the arrest of the two suspects later that night by the police. These individuals were linked to several other robberies in the area. The police department encourages everyone to report any suspicious activity they may observe, even if they think it's nothing. If it wasn't for the alert citizen in the above story, these criminals may have never been apprehended.

Identifying Risks:
Neighbors play an important part in your overall crime prevention program. The purpose of the Neighborhood Watch Program is to help reduce crime and fear of crime in our neighborhoods. The program helps to ensure a prompt and effective response to neighborhood crime and serves to promote positive communication and relationships within a neighborhood.

In the above incident, the citizen was not aware a crime had been committed or one was being committed at the time of his or her observation. They simply observed activity that was suspicious in nature and chose to report that suspicious activity to the police. Neighborhood Watch Programs work because people want to assume a more active role in making their communities safe. While it would be impractical to place a law enforcement officer into each neighborhood, it is very practical to utilize residents to notice and prevent crime. This is why most police departments have a crime alert program to ensure their residents have a way of finding out the type and location of crimes, and the ability to report critical information as soon as possible.

Time and accuracy are critical in reporting crime or suspicious events. Use your law enforcement agency's emergency number to report life-threatening incidents or a crime in progress, and use the non-emergency number for crimes that have already occurred. Your call could save a life, prevent an injury, or stop a crime. The information you provide will be kept confidential. You do not even need to give your name, although it is often helpful.

Residents within a neighborhood usually know who belongs there and who doesn't. They also know what activity is suspicious. Instead of relying on law enforcement to combat crime in their community, neighbor's form a partnership with the local law enforcement that creates positive community teamwork. When you call to report suspicious persons of activity, you not only aid the police, you make your community a safer place to live as well. Some people fail to call the police simply because they are not aware of what might be suspicious. Other people notice suspicious activity and hesitate to call for fear of being labeled as "nosey" or a "pest." Others feel that someone else may have already called the police. Neighborhood Watch Programs help citizens unite and put these hesitations aside. They give each neighborhood and house within that neighborhood, a voice that will be listened to by law enforcement.

As the number of success stories about Neighborhood Watch Programs increases, more and more communities have adopted the program. Thirty-four years have passed since Neighborhood Watch Programs first began. It continues to evolve and expand to encompass more than just neighborhood concerns.

As we all spend time in our neighborhoods, we realize how important it is that everybody cares about the security of their house and follows simple security measures. When a burglar is driving around a neighborhood and sees homeowners leaving their garage doors open all the time, they see opportunity. The security of your neighbor's home is linked to the security of your home. If their home is not burglar-proof, then a burglar might spend more time evaluating your neighborhood. Burglars tend to avoid neighborhoods that are collectively security conscious. Do not let them think your neighborhood is vulnerable.

Tips:

Recognize suspicious activity:

- Be alert. Anything that seems slightly "out of place" or is occurring at an unusual time of day could be criminal activity.

- Do not attempt to apprehend a person committing a crime or to investigate a suspicious activity. Call the police or sheriff's department immediately, and do not worry about being embarrassed if your suspicions prove to be unfounded. Law enforcement officers would rather investigate than be called when it is too late.

The below actions could indicate criminal activity:

- Continuous repair operations at a non-business location could indicate stolen property being altered.

- Open or broken doors and windows at a closed business or unoccupied residence may have been caused by burglary or vandalism.

- Unusual noises, such as gunshots, screaming, or dogs barking continuously are possibly signs of burglary, assault or rape.
- The sound of breaking glass could mean a burglary or vandalism.

Suspicious Persons:

- Groups going door to door in a residential area. Especially if one or more people go to the rear of the residence or loiter in front of an unoccupied house or closed business. This could be a potential burglary.
- Individuals forcing entrance or entering an unoccupied house could mean burglary, theft, or trespassing.
- A person running, especially if carrying something of value or carrying unwrapped property at an unusual hour, could mean a perpetrator is fleeing from a crime.
- Heavy traffic to and from a residence, particularly if it occurs on a daily basis, could mean that the resident is selling drugs or stolen property.
- A person exhibiting unusual mental or physical symptoms may indicate that a person may be injured, under the influence of drugs, or otherwise needing medical attention.

Securing Smiles

Securing Smiles

Chapter 7: Making Your Park Visit Safe.

An unidentified man assaulted a 10-year-old girl in the girls' bathroom in a park. After the assault, the suspect left the bathroom and ran southbound in front of the park office and continued in an unknown direction of travel.

Identifying Risks:

The above example illustrates how dangerous a park can be. You must know where your child is at all times. Escort your child to the bathroom because bathrooms are desired places for child predators to operate. Bathrooms give obscurity and are usually dark and secluded where it would be easy for crime to happen. Police usually don't take the time to patrol the bathroom and it's easily accessible by potential criminals.

In the United States, we have many beautiful public and private parks and community areas. We have wooded parks and urban athletic parks that have something for all family members. These areas offer many activities which do not cost a lot of money. But what you must remember is that they also can be hunting grounds for people with ill intentions or meeting grounds for illegal activities. How is a park judged to be safe?

One way is to look at the crime statistics around the neighborhood of the park. The local law enforcement website should offer reported criminal incidents on a visual map or on a crime chart. This is an easy way to increase public awareness of criminal activity. In addition, it allows citizens to be proactive about the areas they choose to visit or avoid. Increasing numbers of people are expressing concern for their personal safety in urban settings. Some people feel afraid to use public spaces and public facilities. But as I have stated previously, being proactive is a must when it comes to you and your family's personal security. Do your homework and check out the park before you visit.

Crime statistics are not the only factors to assess crime. How is the park managed? Do they have security and if they do what type? Is it clean, is it landscaped? Is the equipment in good condition? All these questions tie into the proper running of a park. Even city parks that normally do not have staff on-site have a responsibility to ensure the city property is maintained. Neglect or mismanagement of park services and facilities can be the first warning sign that crime may be present. Crime is most likely to happen in the dark or in secluded areas. At night, if the park is not well lit you may want to wait until daylight or use a gym facility. You have the right to be choosy.

If you are at the park and someone is hanging around watching the children and not with a child, be suspicious. Ask other parents or guardians at the park if they know that person and work with other parents to ensure that person does not mean to do harm. Call the police if you become suspicious, but do not approach the person. That person may have a weapon, so be cautious but proactive.

Tips:

- Have your cell phone charged and ensure you have cellular coverage while you are at the park.

- Be cautious of persons asking to take photos of your child. If you notice someone taking pictures of your child, leave the area. A person with a legitimate reason will ask permission and show you identification.

- Limit texting or cell phone usage because this distracts from attention to your child or children. Be observant of your children while at the park. Do not get distracted.

- Choose your park wisely by conducting research about past criminal activity in and or around the park. Ensure neighborhood of park is safe.

- Know where security services or the information desk is located.

- Beware of poorly lit areas if visiting at night.

- Look for information about park layout, location of telephones and to whom problems can be reported.

- Know what your child is wearing and discuss a plan if he or she gets separated from you.

- Do not wear expensive jewelry or carry a purse.

- If visiting a national park or a park with trails, do not go off and explore unless you are with a group.

- Do not leave valuables in your car while you are in the park.

Securing Smiles

Chapter 8: Keeping Your Eyes Open At The Mall.

I walked into the police substation which was located on the second floor inside the shopping mall. As I was waiting to speak to the detective about an investigation I was working on, I noticed a picture board that had many pictures of young adults on it. One picture stood out. It was a picture of a young pretty teenage girl with long blonde hair and a very sad expression on her face. She had a date written on her picture written in red ink. I asked the detective what the red ink mean and he said that was the date she died of a drug overdose.

Turns out, the girl was from a neighboring suburban city who the detective said apparently felt like an outcast in her world and ventured out to find someone who she could connect with. She met a young man while at the mall who introduced her to a life of stealing, prostitution and drugs. She got in way over her head and died as a result.

The detective told me that it is a sad reality that this does happen at all malls across the country. He said that parents need to understand when their teenager goes to the mall by themselves; they have to understand that there are dangers at the mall.

Identifying Risks:
The above scenario is a sad case about types of behavior and criminal happenings our kids may be subjected to at the mall. This represents why children and teenagers need to be taught what to do if they find themselves in a dangerous situation. Do these happen frequently? In my opinion no they probably do not. But, like crime, it can happen and you must be prepared

to teach your teenager how to identify risks and avoid them. They need to know that there are people and other teenagers committing crimes at the mall and know how to stay clear of them. Teens, more times than not, carry cash and tend to be less aware of the many money scams there are. Teens can easily get distracted and oblivious to the surrounding around them. They need to be taught the basics of what to do and where to go for help. Since we are in the cell phone age, they need to keep their cell phone charged and not let it be a distracter when they are in the public. They need to feel comfortable to be able to talk to their parents about their individual safety while at the mall or with friends. They need to be educated on what is safe and what is not.

As we all have gone to malls, we know that they are a melting pot of different kinds and types of people. Not only is it a great place to watch different kinds of people, but it can be a wonderful opportunity for criminals because of the lack of shoppers paying attention. Again using the scenario above, it is an atmosphere with many people who have different objectives and reasons for being at the mall. Most are shopping looking for deals or going to their favorite store. Some are walking for the exercise. No matter what your business is at the mall, we all must be aware. Along with teaching our teens to be aware about the above scenario, we also have to teach them about predator's that hang out at malls looking for their next victim.

Predators may approach a potential victim seeking directions or need or offer some kind of assistance. With map in hand a predator may very nicely ask, "I'm lost. Can you please help me?" or, "Can you please tell me how to find Ron's Photo Shop?" Trust your gut. It could be a ploy to size you up. Don't hesitate or delay in order to assist them. Ignore them and quickly resist your urge to want to help. Make sure that you are not being followed. The predator may try to draw attention to a problem with your vehicle like a flat tire, broken light or a fluid leak or create some other story to divert your attention. If you are put in this situation, try to be cordial, but if he or she does not listen, do not be afraid to run and scream for help. Remember, it is your life and if you are with your children, their safety depends on your decisions and actions.

As we have discussed, a mall is not a place to let your guard down. Shoppers, especially adults responsible for children, cannot assume that a mall is safe. When visiting malls, family members must understand and practice basic security protocols. Be alert and know what is going on around you. Watch your children and do not become preoccupied when in stores or walking. Children, make easy targets. If your child got separated from you at a mall, would he or she know how to ask a stranger for help or would your child wait to be approached? We need to teach them what to look for when seeking help from an adult. One recommendation is that children should be instructed to look for a family or a mother with children and ask them for help. In addition, we need to point out safe people and places at a mall including police officers, security guards and the information desk. I think you would agree, not all strangers are bad people; on the contrary, most strangers are generally good people and want to do the right thing.

Tips:

Security While Shopping:

- Stay alert and be aware of what's going on around you.

- Park in a well lit space, as close to the store entrance as possible and away from dumpsters, bushes, or large vehicles. Be sure to lock your doors, close windows, and hide shopping bags and gifts in the trunk.

- Never leave your car unoccupied with the motor running or with children inside. A car can be stolen in seconds.

- Avoid carrying large amounts of cash; pay with a credit card whenever possible but make sure you watch the person handling your credit card. Don't let them walk away with your card and make sure they only swipe it once in front of you.

- Carry your keys, cash, and credit cards separate from each other.

- Remember exactly where you parked your car. Make a mental note or write it down so you will know.

- Teach children to go to a store clerk or security guard if you get separated. Also, have a family "code word" in case you get separated. This word can be given to security staff so that your child can discern friend from foe.

- Carry bags close to your body and ensure you have strong straps and a secure zipper (that are zipped) or snaps (that are snapped.) Sometimes the most secure bag is not the most fashionable, but my wife tells me they exist.

- Shop with another adult so you can take turns browsing and minding the children.

- Keep children close by at all times and do not let them wander around unsupervised.

- Emphasize the importance to your child of

staying close to you.

- If you take packages out to your vehicle and then plan to return to the stores to do more shopping, it may be a good idea to move your car to another section of the parking lot or street.

- If you think you are being followed to your car, do not go back to your car. Return to the safety of the occupied shopping area or office buildings and contact the authorities.

Tips you need to share with your teens about safety in the mall:

- Use the buddy system do and not let them go alone. Even going to the bathroom.

- Make sure they stay aware of their surroundings when they are in the mall and when they are entering and exiting a store.

- Don't flash cash or credit cards.

- Wear appropriate clothing.

- Know where to go for help if needed and keep cell phone charged up.

- Talk to your local law enforcement in the area of the mall so you can find out what crimes are happening in the mall you frequent. This can be a great teaching aid to use for communicating to your teenager the risks at the mall.

ATM security checklist:

- Select an ATM located near the center of a building not at the corner of a building. Corners create a blind area that is in close proximity to the customer's transaction and reduces the effective reaction time by the user.

- Select an ATM located near the center of a building.

- Select an ATM at a location that is in plain sight and the view is not blocked behind shrubbery, landscaping, signs or decorative partitions or dividers. Watch out for any type of hiding areas for would-be assailants.

- Select an ATM that is in a well lit location.

- Whenever possible, select an ATM that is monitored or patrolled by a security officer.

- Select an ATM with a wide angle transaction camera and/ or a continuous transaction surveillance camera. Consult the bank or location management for this information.

- Solicit prior criminal activity statistics from law enforcement for the ATM site and surrounding neighborhood.

- Maintain an awareness of your surroundings throughout the entire area.

- Do not wear expensive jewelry.

- Be aware of anyone sitting in a parked car in close proximity to, or at a distance from the ATM location.

- When leaving, make sure you are not being followed.

- Shield the ATM keypad from anyone who may be standing or parked nearby or anyone crowding you in an attempt to view your transaction. This may be an attempt to determine your PIN, or they may be waiting for you.

- ATM's can be a gold mine for criminals because the money taken out is non-traceable and people usually are unaware of their surroundings. So be aware.

Chapter 9: Is Your Child's Identity Safe?

An ex-Girl Scout Troop Leader was charged with 19 counts of filing false claims and 15 counts of identity theft last fall after creating fraudulent medical forms for members of her Girl Scout troop and asking parents to fill them out and return them to her. She used the information to file bogus tax returns and collect $87,000 in illegal tax refunds, which were then distributed into five different bank accounts, according to the U.S. Attorney's office and documents filed in the United States District Court, North Florida District. She was sentenced to 10 years in prison.

Identifying Risks:

What would you do if your child's identity was stolen? In the above scenario, a trusted Girl Scout Leader used fraudulent medical forms to get private information from her troop members. Luckily, she was caught and now the families can begin fixing their child's identity. But what happens if it is stolen for years and you may not be aware of it? As I have discussed throughout this book, we worry a lot about our children and will do whatever we can to protect them. We monitor their friends, what they eat, their health, their school, and their cell phone use. We monitor everything. Something that may never even cross our mind is the need to protect them from identity theft.

According to the FTC, over 20,000 kids were victims of identity theft in 2008. This number only includes those thefts that were actually reported. There were probably more who didn't report the identity theft to the FTC or maybe don't even know they've been victimized yet. Identity theft is a problem and continues to grow every year.

Your child's credit history should be clear and ready for him or her to build a solid credit standing as an adult. But, how many times have you checked your children's credit history? If your teenager applies for a credit card, a cell phone or a student loan, you may have gotten a credit history check. Some people are finding out once their children apply for one of the above, they are already deep into credit debt that is not even theirs. Plus, the burden is on them to prove they are innocent. Even though it seems obvious that a ten-year-old didn't take out a loan to buy a condo in Arizona, you'd be surprised at just how hard it is to clear his or her name. Identity theft protection is critical in this day and age of electronic finances.

One problem we did not have when I was a child or teen was the internet. Does your child or teen visit many different social-networking sites? Some sites will allow only a particular community of users to access posted content. Others allow everybody to view postings. Understand what sites your children are visiting and what information they are posting. Limit the sites you allow your child to visit and restrict access to a select group of people, such as their buddies from school, a club, a team or a community group. Tell your child to never post online his or her full name, age, social security number, address, and phone number or bank and credit card account numbers. Make sure your child's screen name doesn't say too much about him or her. Remember, once your child's information is posted online, they cannot take it back. Even if deleted, old versions of the information still exist on other people's computers.

We must be vigilant in protecting our children's future. If someone insists they need your child's social security number or personal information, verify that they really need it. Both my wife and I have refused to give out my family's social security numbers to be used as patient identification numbers even at the doctor's office. When we explain our reason for refusing, most staff members have understood. I reiterate, before giving your child's information to anybody, ask yourself if they really need it. It is probably not essential for them to have. Your child's identity is with them for life, so do your best to ensure they have a fresh and clean beginning.

Tips:

- Don't let kids carry their social security cards in their wallets. These cards should always be stored in a safe place.

- Keep your child's magazine subscriptions under your name, not his or hers. This helps prevent your child's name from appearing on mailing lists.

- Pay attention if your child starts receiving junk mail. If your twelve-year-old suddenly begins receiving credit card invitations in her name, it may mean that her personal information has been compromised or it may be an innocent marketing tool sent by an affiliate of your bank because you opened a college fund for your child. A quick check of credit reports will help you sort out the truth.

Child identity theft often is detected when young people:

- Are unable to open a bank or checking account.

- Receive collection notices in the mail or by telephone.

- Are denied driver's license renewal.

- Are quoted higher than normal insurance rates.

- Have been receiving bills or credit cards they never requested, perhaps for years.

- Are notified by a law enforcement agency investigating a large case in which they happen to be a part of.

- Are arrested for an activity they never committed.

- Are denied social security income or welfare services.

- Receive numerous pre-approved credit card offers come in the mail in the name of the child.

- Receive credit cards, checks, bills or bank statements.

- Are contacted by collection agencies calling or sending letters about accounts not opened by the child.

- Are denied the right to get a driver's license because another person has a license with that social security number as identification. The imposter may even have accumulated tickets or citations in the child's name.

- Are contacted by law enforcement with a warrant for an arrest of the child.

If you suspect your child has become the victim of an identity thief, follow these steps:

- Get a copy of your child's credit record. You can request a free copy from the three major credit reporting agencies by going to www. annualcredit report.com or calling 1-877-322-8228. You can also request that a fraud alert be placed on your child's file, which will prevent identity thieves from opening any more accounts in your child's name.

- Get a copy of your child's social security statement, which you can obtain at www.ssa. gov/mystatement/ or by calling 1-800-772-1213. This statement will help you determine if anyone has used your child's social security number to get a job or obtain government benefits.

- File a police report. You will likely need a copy of a police report to show creditors.

- Report the theft to the Federal Trade Commission (FTC) by using their online complaint form or calling the 1-877-ID-THEFT. The FTC supports law enforcement officials as they track down and stop identity thieves.

- Contact creditors listed on your child's credit record, notifying them of the situation and asking them to close the account. You will probably need to complete a fraud affidavit for each creditor. The FTC provides a uniform affidavit form, which is available at www.ftc.gov/bcp/conline/pubs/credit/affidavit.pdf.

While you complete the above steps, make sure you:

- Keep a log of all phone conversations, dates, times, names, phone numbers, and topic of discussion.

- Track your time and expenses.

- Confirm the results of conversations in writing.

- Send correspondence by certified mail, return receipt requested.

- Keep copies of all letters and documents you send.

Chapter 10: Is The Cyber Wild West Safe For Your Children?

According to authorities, a man has been charged with sexually assaulting a teenager he met in an internet chat room. A 17-year-old told police she met a 56- year-old man on the internet and met him at a fast-food restaurant. They went to a liquor store. The man bought beer, tequila and vodka. At his home the girl drank alcohol, got drunk, vomited, and he began touching her. She told police she tried to get up, but he held her down and then she passed out. When she woke up there were signs that she had been sexually assaulted.

Identifying Risks:

Cyberspace is a gigantic community hosting millions of people. It is a place where people research information for school, learn about movies, shop, listen to music, watch video clips, and develop sites of their own. It is the new Wild West with very little protection from people who are very good at manipulating and retrieving your data. As in any community, there are types of people you should avoid and be aware to protect everyone in your family. In the above example, a 56-year-old man preyed on a teenager. The teen agreed to a meeting and was assaulted after the adult got her intoxicated.

Parents can take some simple steps to protect their children or teenagers from online invasion by these predators. Become more aware of what your children are doing online. Check in once in a while to actually see where they go on the internet. Tell your children not to chat with adult strangers without supervision and never fill out a personal information profile for any site. It is best not to open unsolicited email or email from strangers. This mail could be a cover to sell or provide online pornography or criminal activity. If your child received pornography via the internet or someone has made inappropriate contact with your child, contact your local police.

According to the FTC, an estimated 15.8 million children are using the internet today. By 2010, approximately 16.6 million kids will be online. With so many children online, today's predators can easily find and exploit them. For predators, the internet is a new, effective, and more anonymous way to seek out and groom children for criminal purposes.

Whether your child is studying or socializing online, parents need to make smart choices to keep them safe. Among the many choices we are faced with online is how to deal with their personal information. The Children's Online Privacy Protection Act (COPPA) gives parents control over what information websites can collect from their kids. Any website for kids under thirteen, or any other site that collects personal information from kids which it knows are under thirteen, is required to comply with COPPA. The FTC, which is the nation's consumer protection agency, enforces this law. According to COPPA, web sites must obtain parent's permission before collecting or sharing your child's personal information. That includes information websites that ask for information before you can use the website and information your kids choose to post about themselves on websites. Personal information includes your child's full name, address, email address, or cell phone number.

Let's face it, who doesn't use email nowadays. When was the last time you actually wrote a letter using a pen and paper? Email is a great way to communicate with your friends and family whether if they are in India or Indiana. You receive many different types of emails. Sometimes you may receive messages trying to sell you something or encouraging you to visit a website. Do not to respond to email from people or groups you don't know. These sites might be a scam to sell you something you don't want. Remember, the sender might not be who he or she seems to be. If you respond, you are confirming that you have a valid email address. That information can encourage the sender to forward inappropriate email or put your address on even more junk email lists.

Chat rooms are like having a bunch of people in your living room talking about a subject that everybody is interested in. But think about it, why are they interested in that subject. Is it because the subject interests them or are they interested in knowing more about you. That is something you do not know. You could be chatting with a serial killer, rapist or a child abductor. You do not know.

The anonymity of a chat room can be liberating and mysterious for children. But make no mistake, it also can be deadly. The following CBS News report is an example of a deadly confrontation: A thirteen-year-old moved to live with her aunt because her parents had substance abuse problems. At her private school, the 6th-grader had good grades, led the cheerleading squad and was an altar girl. On the internet, she used provocative screen names and routinely met and had sex with partners she met in chat rooms. Only months after moving, she was strangled by a twenty-five-year-old married man. The girl had met him on the internet and met him in person several times before he killed her. He confessed and led police to her body in a remote ravine in the city he lived in.

A child or teenager should never meet

face to face with somebody they have met on the internet. The only exception is if the parent knows the person or is going along to chaperone the meeting.

Never say anything in a chat room that you wouldn't say in public. Many chat rooms have monitors or speakers who maintain order. These monitors can kick people out of the room for inappropriate behavior. If you meet someone online and strike up a good relationship with them, they may want to go to a private chat room. Most private rooms are unmonitored. There will be no filter for inappropriate conduct.

The internet is an extraordinary world where you can nearly find anything imaginable. But, do not forget, anything can also find you. Be careful, monitor your children's computer usage and censor if needed. You need to know what your kids are doing on the computer.

Tips:

Parent web safety tips for their children:

- Never give out your name, address, telephone number, password, school name, parent's name, pictures of yourself, credit card numbers, or any other personal information to others online.

- Never agree to meet face to face with someone you've met online without discussing it with your parents. If your parents decide that it's okay to meet your cyber-friend, arrange to meet in a familiar public place and take a trusted adult with you.

- Never respond to messages from unfamiliar persons.

- Never enter an area that charges for services without getting your parents' permission first.

- If you receive pornographic material or threatening email, save the offensive material, tell your parents, and contact your local law enforcement agency and that user's internet service provider.

Internet facts:

- **Adolescence 18 years and younger spend an average of 18 hours per week online.** *National Crime Prevention Council, March 2008*

- **One in five children receives an unwanted sexual solicitation online each year.** Solicitations were defined as requests to engage in sexual activities or sexual talk, or to give personal sexual information. *Crimes Against Children Research Center.* Websites that children visit very often are also cruised by child predators. "My Cyber Crimes Unit investigators have seen firsthand the dangerous criminals that prey on children and teenagers in internet chat rooms, personal web pages, and social networking sites." *Texas Attorney General Greg Abbott*

- **Seventy-seven percent of the targets for online predators were age 14 or older. Another 22% were users ages 10 to 13.** *Crimes Against Children Research Center*

Securing Smiles

Chapter 11: A Teamwork Approach In Making Schools Safe.

An adult male entered the school through an unofficial entrance. The man asked a teacher for directions to the student office. As he began walking towards the student office, several students believed they saw the adult male carrying a gun. School security procedures were followed and the adult male was arrested immediately and without incident by the school liaison officer and removed from the school. The adult male was found to be carrying a replica gun. Staff and students were praised for their quick and decisive reaction to the incident.

District officials say the door the man used to gain access to the high school is locked from the outside, and that visitors have to be buzzed in. That suggests that a student either let the man in, or that he slipped in behind someone.

Identifying Risks:

The above scenario illustrates how important the need for a school security plan is and how important it is that school staff members understand and follow it. The question that needs to be addressed is how did a man with a gun get into the school? The school had emergency procedures in place, fluid communication by students and decisive action taken by staff and the schools police officer. But still, how did the man get into the school?

Schools need to control who is coming in to their schools. This is not an easy task. There are many people who have valid reasons for visiting a school. You want your school to be a place people can visit, but there needs to be access controls in place. A school needs a strong visitor-management policy that can help keep unwanted persons off school grounds. At a minimum, all visitors should be required to check in at the school office. Another example is to have one door in the front of the school open that funnels all traffic to the main office or reception office. This office will have a staff person whose responsibility is to check all visitors and grant or deny entry.

Schools should also include a visitor badging system along with all school employees wearing an identification badge. After signing in at the office, all visitors should receive a temporary credential to wear while on the school property. This makes it easier to notice if an adult is wearing a visitor badge or an employee identification badge. If a person is not wearing a badge, they need to be challenged appropriately. Parents need to be aware of the security measures at their child's school.

As a parent of a child in school and hearing that a man got into a school with a gun is extremely concerning. But what if the attacker came from the student population? As the terrible events in Arkansas and many other instances in recent times illustrate, it only takes one distressed student to cause horrific violence. Some children can get angry very quickly when a teacher is insistent that rules will be followed for the good of all. The early identification and intervention of behavior abnormalities in students who may have a tendency towards violence must be acted upon quickly so the unthinkable act can be averted. Counseling of staff is critical. Find out your child's school policy so you know what to do if your child comes home and he or she was threatened by a peer or tells you he or she witnessed a threatening behavior. Some questions you should ask your school officials are:

- Is your school staff prepared to deal with a disgruntled student or fired staff member?

- How does your school identify and deal with children who are exhibiting threatening behaviors? Furthermore, how do teachers or administrative staff monitor and report kids that show disturbing behaviors?

- How do I report threatening behavior if my son or daughter tells me?

- What is your school's policy for a student who threatens another child or threatens a teacher? Is it suspension or expulsion?

- Are lockdown drills completed on a consistent basis to ensure everybody knows what to do?

- What policies are in place to prevent an unauthorized person from walking into your school?

Preparing a school to respond to a serious incident is a difficult task. But the good thing is our schools are not alone in planning and executing the security plan. Local law enforcement plays a part in coordinating a security program with the schools. They assist by enforcing the laws in schools and supporting the creation and execution of emergency policy procedures. A school-law enforcement partnership is a process rather than an event. Partnerships do not just happen when a law enforcement officer is assigned to a school, but are built on a foundation of shared goals, ongoing communication, and positive relationships. When schools and law enforcement agencies work together and in concert with other community-based organizations, parents and students, a number of positive outcomes can be expected:

- Schools, law enforcement agencies, and

community groups are better able to work together in developing innovative, system wide, long-term approaches to reducing and preventing different kinds of crime and disorder in and around their school.

- Schools and law enforcement agencies can have measurable impacts on targeted crime and disorder.

- Duplication of efforts is reduced.

- Students, school personnel, parents, and community members have less fear of crime and violence.

- Schools and communities show improved quality of life.

Although the roles of schools and law enforcement agencies differ, there are some significant areas of commonality. First, for law enforcement agencies, working within the schools is a logical extension into the school setting of their responsibilities for public safety in the broader community. Second, both schools and law enforcement agencies can play an important role in helping youth to become productive, law-abiding citizens. Both set and reinforce expectations for behavior associated with good citizenship such as honesty and consideration for others. Additionally, law enforcement officers complement the school's educational mission by conducting law-related educational activities that teach the rights and responsibilities of citizenship. Community policing in schools supports and reinforces good citizenship in students by approaching schools as neighborhoods and students as citizens.

Teamwork is important between schools, law enforcement and parents. The following is an example of the three entities working together to strengthen security for our children:

Securing Smiles

As my wife and I drove into the parking lot of my son's school, I noticed there were a bunch of men dressed in jeans and white shirts doing landscape work across the street at the city park. Being a veteran of the prison system and knowing that this is kind of an odd uniform, I had a strong suspicion they were inmates. Upon driving around the block, I notice their foreman next to the government van supervising their work. I walked back into the school and told the director that there were ten to twelve inmates working right next to the school. She looked surprised and told me she would look into it right away.

Wanting to get a better understanding, the director immediately communicated the situation to her school board, and set up a meeting to talk to the Chief of Police of the city the school was in. The Chief confirmed they were county low security inmates contracted to do work for the city. He also said they were low security inmates that have been screened closely and are supervised by an officer.

The director questioned the Chief on why the school was not notified they had convicted felons working right across the street from young vulnerable children. The director then told the Chief that she is not comfortable with the inmates working in such a close vicinity to her school. The chief agreed and changed the group's work detail to a different location.

As the above example illustrates, parents need to be aware of where they are dropping off their children or where the bus is taking their children. If they see a problem or something out of the ordinary, do not be afraid to bring it to the school's administration attention. I did, and the school official acted right away and took care of the situation. A parents responsibility is to provide the necessary due diligence for their children, which means not only researching the school before hand, but paying attention while they are going to school. As my attorney wife often states, "We are our children's voice and we are their advocate. That is not a responsibility we can delegate."

Ninety-nine percent of educators are incredible leaders and pillars of the community who would do anything to keep their students safe. They have a tough job to do. I want to reassure parents that according to the U.S. Department of Education, school-age children are nine times more likely to sustain an unintentional injury than to be the victim of violence while at school. I believe our schools our safe. We need to support our teachers and our school. By being responsible and proactive parents, we assist educators in being able to teach our children better and keep them safer. This is what teamwork is all about.

Tips:

School Parent Security Assessment: (U.S. Dept of Education)

- **Ask your child about safety in his or her school**. This will allow you to see if he or she is paying attention and, hopefully, he or she will be able to tell you about safety drills.

- **Identify comfort levels and methods for reporting safety concerns**. Does your child have at least one adult they would feel comfortable in reporting safety concerns to at school?

- **Examine access to your school**. Are there a reduced number of doors that can be accessed from the outside, while still allowing children to exit from the inside for an emergency?

- **Find out if your school has policies and procedures on security and emergency preparedness.** Does your board and administration have written policies and procedures related to security, crisis preparedness planning, and overall school safety planning?

- **Determine if your school has a "living" school safety team, a working safety plan, as well as a school crisis team and school emergency/crisis preparedness guidelines.** Does your school have a school safety committee to develop an overall plan for prevention, intervention, and security issues?

- **Inquire with school and public safety officials as to whether school officials use internal security specialists and outside public safety resources to develop safety plans and crisis guidelines.** Do school officials have meaningful, working relationships with police, fire and other public safety agencies serving their schools?

- **Ask if school emergency/crisis guidelines are tested and exercised.** Do school officials test and exercise written crisis guidelines? What type of tests do they perform?

- **Determine whether school employees, including support personnel, have received training on school security and crisis preparedness issues.** Have school employees received training on security and emergency strategies by local, state and national specialists? Have employees also received training on their school district specific crisis guidelines? Are all employees, including support personnel such as secretaries and custodians, included in such training? How often is such training provided? Is the training provided by qualified and experienced instructors with knowledge of K-12 specific safety issues?

- **Find out if school officials use outside resources and sources in their ongoing school safety assessments.** Do school officials subscribe to current publications addressing security issues? Do they attend conferences and programs on school safety? Have they reviewed their security measures, crisis guidelines and safety plans with recommendations by school safety experts?

- **Parents need to be involved and play a part and evaluate whether as a parent, they are doing their part in making schools safe.** Do they follow parking, visitor, and other safety procedures at your school? Do they support teachers and administrators with safety initiatives, including by asking the above questions in a supportive, non-blaming manner? Do they talk with their child about personal safety considerations, drug and violence prevention issues, and related topics early and regularly at home? Do they seek professional help for their child in a timely manner, if needed?

Chapter 12: Is My Child's Organization Safe?

As I sat in the conference room, waiting to listen to our little league baseball commissioner speak on the upcoming baseball season, a women came to my row and asked all the baseball coaches to give her their drivers license so she could start the background process. I pulled my license out of my wallet and gave her my license.

Identifying Risks:

One thing each parent loves to do is get his or her child involved in an extracurricular activity. Baseball, soccer, Boy Scouts, Girl Scouts, hockey, to name a few, are great activities for your child's self esteem and confidence. This is how our kids grow and learn rules and learn how to work as a team. The kids also have fun.

But as Spiderman's Uncle wisely stated, "With great powers comes great responsibility." Before signing your child up for activities, you need to check out the group or organization to ensure it is legitimate and safe for your child. You must understand how each organization is run and you need to be informed of their control measures during the hiring process. In the above example, I volunteered to coach a youth baseball team. The baseball organizations policy was to run a background check on each coach. A parent must ensure the organization they are signing their child up for has a background reviewing process in their hiring procedures. Remember this is your child and you are entrusting other adults to have complete control over your children when you are not around.

Every day, tens of millions of U.S. children access the resources and support network of nonprofit organizations. Nonprofits need volunteers and staff members to help them provide a valuable service to these children. However, in this era, finding volunteers with time is now a challenge. Nonprofit organizations are finding themselves in a difficult position and are sometimes desperate to find assistance. This can lead to acceptance of applicants with criminal records who fall through the cracks and are offered a position where they are working with children.

According to the Bureau of Labor statistics, about 61.8 million people or 26.4 percent of the population in the U.S. volunteered for an organization at least once between September 2007 and September 2008. According to the National Center for Charitable Statistics, the number of nonprofit organizations in the United States has grown to 1.4 million. The Bureau of Labor also reported that annual volunteer hours were the second highest at youth oriented organizations, second only to religious groups.

Tips:

What you need to know and do before your child joins an organization:

- Do they publish their telephone number and address so they are easily reached?

- Do they have any awards for child safety or education?

- Are they endorsed by people you trust such as the government or child safety organizations?

- Are they approved by your child's school or other parents?

- Do they conduct background checks on each organization employee or volunteer who is in contact with your child?

- Check your Secretary of State's office to ensure the organization is a legitimate non-profit organization and is in good standing.

- Attend organizational events with your child and do not leave him or her in their care until you feel comfortable.

- Ensure open communication with your children so they will tell you if something is troubling them about the organization.

- Ask the organization for a copy of their security/safety policy. They should have one. If not, ask them to discuss their emergency procedures.

- If something does not feel right about the organization, take your child out immediately and contact the appropriate authorities.

- Meet the employees before the event begins so you get to know them and develop a rapport with them.

- Give your child (if old enough) a cell phone to call you if he or she need you.

Securing Smiles

Chapter 13: Staying Safe While In Your Vehicle

A young woman was coming home from her parent's cabin with her 1 year old twins after a long day of fishing. It was dark and the young mom was extremely tired. As she was traveling down the highway, she noticed a car was parked ahead of her and a person was trying to signal her down. She knew better then to pick up a hitch-hiker so she did not stop. It was apparent to her that this man ran out of gas or was having some sort of car troubles. Because she was not sure what his problem was and knew the man was not hurt, she got out her cell phone and called road side assistance and gave them his location.

Identifying Risks:

When you are driving in your vehicle it is important that you practice common sense security. When you are traveling with children, common sense security needs to be heightened because there is an increased risk due to your precious cargo. In the above example, the woman knew better than to stop and help the man. She saw him waiting by the road next to a parked car trying to wave her down for assistance. Her eyes saw a man looking for assistance, but what did her instincts see?

I know from the scary movie hysteria that you are also thinking the broken down car could have been a ploy to either carjack her car or assault her or her children. Yes, that could have been the result. There also could have been an accomplice lying on the other side of the road waiting to attack her when she stopped and her attention was on his buddy. Yes you are right, things like that can happen. But chances are he simply had car trouble. No matter why this per-

79

son was stopped on the road, the woman did the right thing by keeping her vehicle moving and calling for assistance. She was driving with her two small children and was not obligated to put herself and her children in danger by stopping to assist a stranger.

When traveling in your vehicle, it is important to be aware of what type of neighborhood or areas you are in. As a rule, when your family or you are traveling in your car, always keep the doors locked. Any time you drive through areas containing stoplights, stop signs, or anything that significantly reduces your vehicle's speed, keep your windows up. Leave ample maneuvering space between your vehicle and the one in front of you. This allows you to drive away if approached by a suspicious person. In addition, if you are approached by a suspicious person while you are stopped, do not roll down windows; drive away quickly. If you are being followed or harassed by another driver, try to find the nearest police station, hotel, or other public facility. Once you find a place of safety, don't worry about using a legal parking space. Park as close as you can to the entrance and get inside fast.

If another driver tries to cut you off or forces you to pull over, keep driving and try to get away. Try to memorize the license plate number of the car and description of the car and driver and report the incident to local law enforcement. This behavior could indicate an impaired driver, so authorities need to get that driver off the streets for the safety of others. If trying to get this information puts you in danger, don't do it. The information is not as important as your safety.

If you are being followed, never lead the person back to your home or stop and get out. Drive to the nearest police station or public facility. If you are traveling alone and a car "bumps" into you, don't stop to exchange accident information if you are not sure of your safety or your instincts tell you something is not right. Go to the nearest service station or other public place to call the police. If you are parked on the street and have trouble, be wary of personal assistance from strangers. Use your cell phone to call a family member, friend or call a repair service for assistance. If you feel threatened by the presence of nearby strangers, lock yourself in your car and blow the horn to attract attention of others.

Tips:

Vehicle security checklist:

- Always have your cell phone charged.
- Know the locations of police, fire departments and hospitals.
- Don't leave valuables inside your vehicle, (i.e. global positioning devices, cell phones, PDA's).
- Lock doors and windows when parked or stopped.
- Keep a half-length distance between the vehicles in front of you.
- Be aware of your surroundings when stopped at traffic signals or stop signs.

Tips to avoid being car-jacked:

- Keep your doors locked and windows up and if traveling with children make sure child window lock is engaged.
- If you must stop at a rest stop when traveling, make sure it is populated and you feel safe. If you have any reservation, do not stop.
- Avoid driving alone, especially at night.

Securing Smiles

- Park carefully, in a well lighted area near an entrance.

- When returning to your vehicle, approach with caution. Have your keys ready and glance underneath and inside. If someone is loitering near your car, avoid them and walk to a safe, well lighted place.

- Don't assist other motorists in low traffic areas. Wave or acknowledge as you drive past, noting their exact location and call authorities for help.

- Don't pull over to read a map if lost unless you are in a public place.

- Stay visible. Car-jackers choose people who won't likely be seen by bystanders.

- Keep your car in good driving condition and prepared for seasonal situations.

Chapter 14: Choosing The Right Parking Lot Or Garage Is Important.

Why do parking lots scare many of us when it comes to violent crime? Perhaps it is because they often seem to be void of people, especially at night. Combined with the fact that many high-rise garage parking lots are designed with security-unfriendly areas such as walls, pillars and elevation changes (where people may be lurking) and we begin to see the reason why our common sense makes us apprehensive. Even large open parking lots like the ones attached to shopping malls can offer a thief or violent predator great visibility to watch for security patrols, escape routes and potential victims.

Identifying Risks:

If you look at the statistics from the Department of Justice, roughly 80% of the criminal acts at shopping centers, strip malls and business offices occur in the parking lot or parking garages. Once crime takes place in an area it is difficult to break the trend. It's interesting to note where strong parking lot security procedures have been implemented, customer use has increased because patrons feel safer. So in other words, if the parking lot or garage you are using is always empty, this may be a sign crime is a problem.

The average criminal is lazy. If an area is not being actively patrolled by law enforcement or by security, they are going to continue committing crimes in that area. I understand this point because I spent ten years working in prison with criminals. If they do not have to move far for potential victims they won't. But there are some things you can do to improve your safety when you park your car.

- Know about the area of the parking garage or lot you are going to park in. Is it located in a high crime area? Is there a sufficient security system (CCTV, active patrolling, well lighted, emergency alarms) in the garage or lot?

- Pay attention. Take the time, as you drive into the parking garage, to determine whether anyone is walking around aimlessly and to make sure you park in a well lighted populated area.

- When driving, take note of how clean the parking area is. Look for graffiti or trash. The parking area management should be proactive in keeping the area clean. If it is not, this could be a sign of a parking area that you should not park in.

It has become blatantly clear over the years that many different types of criminal activities are common in parking areas. Many times parking lots are small, enclosed, deserted spaces with poor lighting. If there is a place for a criminal to commit a mugging, or to steal a car, this is the perfect setting. Allowing people to walk around a deserted area with shadows and darkness looming around them is dangerous and not right. Incidents have occurred in which a woman walking to her car is attacked by someone who jumps out from behind a nearby car to steal her purse, hit her or rape her.

I want to reemphasize the importance of paying attention once you enter a parking lot by with your family or by yourself. Do not let yourself wander. Watch your surroundings. This is an area where people tend to let their guard down and are not thinking about what is around them. Be aware of present dangers and act accordingly. Look to see if there are suspicious people in the area or near your car? Is there a van parked next to your vehicle that wasn't there before? You can also choose to carry self defense weapons such as pepper-spray or other legal items for your safety and security. But if you are choosing a self- defense weapon, it is extremely important that you know how to use it and to have it ready.

Calm, realistic awareness is the beginning step you need when parking. Stay mindful of the tips mentioned below and trust your common sense and you'll be safer going to and from your parking lot destinations.

Tips:

- Look around your vehicle for any suspicious activity. If someone is loitering around your vehicle, walk past until he leaves.

- Carry a whistle or other protective alarm with you.

- Make brief eye contact with persons you encounter.

- Be alert and suspicious of anyone approaching your vehicle to hand out leaflets, ask for donations, etc. Always leave the car window up.

- Do a quick scan of your vehicle's interior, including the back seat, before unlocking the door.

- At night, leave your office or building with others, if possible. If you're alone, have someone from building security escort you.

- Approach your vehicle with your keys already in your hand.

- Change from heels to low flats or even sneakers when leaving work in case you need to run.

- Don't park next to a van's sliding door.
- If possible, park next to entrances or in open and well lighted areas.
- Always roll up windows, close the sunroof and lock the doors before leaving your car.
- Avoid leaving valuables in your car; don't leave your cell phone plugged in to the cigarette lighter and in plain view.
- Trust your instinct. If you do not feel comfortable, ask a security officer to escort you to your vehicle.
- Do not linger around your car. Rather, prepare to enter the car quickly and drive away.
- Keep the doors locked and windows up until you have exited the facility.
- Go out of your way and spend the extra time to park in well traveled, busier areas.
- Make sure you look at the Crime Prevention section of your local police department website or the area police departments you are visiting so you can see what types of crimes are happening in the area.
- A store parking lot can change once it gets dark, so if it is getting late, have a plan. Park in a well lighted location and ask for an escort from to your car from a store supervisor. They will do it because they want your repeat business and they want to be perceived as a family-friendly company.
- Identify entrances and exits when entering a parking facility.
- Keep valuables out of sight before you enter the parking garage or lot.
- Immediately report any suspicious activity to

911 and security.

- Drive slowly and follow the designated routes into and out of the garage.

- If you must leave a key with a parking attendant, leave only your vehicle's ignition key. Don't leave anything attached to it.

- Know yourself and how do you react in a crisis situation. Do you scream, cry or freeze? Have a plan for how you would react if confronted.

- Always think ahead. When out at night, have your keys ready to enter the house or to start the car. Hold your keys so you could defend yourself if needed.

What may be considered a suspicious vehicle:

- A car moving slowly, without lights, following aimless course in any location, including residential streets, schools, and playgrounds could signify a burglar, drug pusher or sex offender.

- A parked or occupied vehicle, containing one or more persons, especially at an unusual hour could be a burglary or robbery in progress.

- A car or truck parked by a business or unoccupied residence, being loaded with valuables could mean a burglary or theft.

- A vehicle containing weapons could be many different types of criminal activity.

- A female or juvenile being forced into a vehicle could mean a kidnapping, assault, or attempted rape is happening.

- A vehicle being used as a shelter for a business transaction, especially around schools or parks, could be signs of a sale of stolen items or drugs.

- A vehicle with someone attempting to forcibly enter it could be a theft in progress.

- Persons detaching mechanical parts or accessories from it are signs of a theft or vandalism.

- A car or truck with objects being thrown from it could indicate a person trying to dispose illegal contraband.

Chapter 15: How Do I Keep My Kid's Safe While Traveling?

A family of four took a summer trip to Brussels, Belgium. They had never been to Brussels and they were excited to see the sites. They flew into Berlin and were taking the train to Brussels. As they were waiting with their entire luggage at the train station, a child with a dirty face and old torn clothing approached them started talking to both of them in broken English. As the whole family was trying to understand what the poor little girl was saying, an older lady came from behind and snatched the father's laptop case that was located to his rear. As the dad finally said no to the little girl, he turned around and noticed his laptop case was gone.

Identifying Risks:

Oh how fun it is to travel with children. My wife and I have flown many times with both of our children beginning right when they were born. The best parental advice for flying with young children is the old boy scout motto, 'Be Prepared.' Know where your children are at all times. Things may get a little hectic when you have to pack sixteen different bags and are running behind schedule, only to face the reality of missing your flight. But remember the cardinal rule: You can replace forgotten items and re-schedule flights, but a child is irreplaceable.

No matter how many kids you have, traveling with children can be a major challenge. You must pay attention to your surroundings. In the example at the beginning of the chapter, the family was traveling internationally and was approached by a scam artist dressed as a poor little girl. Scam artists can prey on families with children because they often use dramatic or heart wrenching tactics to get the family's attention. All their eyes were fixated on that poor little girl and their hearts were bleeding for her. For that split second, they were not paying attention to their surroundings and BAM, the accomplice came and snatched a laptop case. That piece of luggage cannot scream or kick like a person, so it was an easy snatch and run. That family has just been duped.

In this chapter, I want to talk about three proactive duties parents need to perform. I also want to make it clear, I am not offering to babysit your kids on the plane, nor am I going to volunteer to be a nanny while you go to Costa Rica. These three duties are researching your vacation destination, becoming aware of travel scams, and practice safe personal security while on vacation. My mission is to ensure that you do not compromise security for fun. You will still be able to have a fun family vacation and come back to brag to your friends and family of how much fun you had. Having fun and being security conscience is a reality if you just plan and use good old common sense.

Researching your family vacation destination is a must whether you are traveling domestically or internationally. You need to understand the basic rules and principles of traveling. Remember, more times than not, you are going to a place you know a little bit about. You need to understand if it is safe to walk on the streets. Also, you need to know how much the security climate changes at night. There are many free media internet websites you can use to find out this information. It is important that you do not just view one site, but look at a couple of sites so you can get an objective look at all of the information. Since most media outlets are private and can be bias towards a particular side, multiple media site reviews need to be completed and interpreted using the facts on those sites, not opinions. Read the newspaper once you are at your vacation site to see what is happening in the area you are in. It is important to know and understand the political and security climate in the area you are traveling to.

In traveling overseas for your vacation, the U.S. State Department's website is a great asset. It issues travel warnings, public announcements, and travel information sheets. It also provides guidance on nationality and citizenship determination, document issuance, judicial and notary services, third-country representation, and disaster assistance. You will also be able to find information to:

- Identify and understand threats, assess vulnerabilities, determine potential impacts and disseminate timely information to our homeland security partners and U.S. travelers.

- Manage and coordinate the national response to acts of terrorism, natural disasters, or other emergencies.

- Lead national, state, local and private sector efforts to restore services and rebuild communities after acts of terrorism, natural disasters, or other emergencies.

Become aware of travel scams happening domestically and internationally. If it sounds too good to be true, it usually is. You just received a letter promising you two free airline tickets just to come to a seminar on a special travel club. It may make sense to go and at least listen for two free tickets. After further research, you find out that the letter was not completely accurate. You call the 1-800 number they provided and hear a high energy "Knute Rockne" speech on a club that has great hotel rates and cruise rates. The only catch is that you have to pay several thousand dollars to join. Would you take it or pass? Definitely, I recommend you pass on it. The two free tickets are and will never be free there is always a catch. Common sense plays a huge part when dealing with vacation deals.

It is just like researching a contractor or someone who does work for you. Be extremely skeptical about unsolicited email, postcard and phone solicitations saying you've been selected to receive a fabulous vacation or anything free. Take the time to make a call and ask the basic questions. If you are talking to someone internationally be extremely observant and skeptical. Many scams start internationally and prey on the elderly or vulnerable people in the US.

When talking with the sales persons, keep ALL information private, unless you are the one who initiated the call. They do not need it. When I worked in the prison system, one of my responsibilities was to work with many Department of Justice agencies regarding Bureau of Prisons transfers. I received many calls from people who said they were federal agents and they needed confidential information on certain inmates incarcerated at our facility. Like the obligation parents have to their children, I had an obligation to the security of our prison to verify the agent to ensure he or she was who they said they were. I first asked for a callback number, office address and their supervisor's name. Second, I checked the number in my federal database to ensure both phone number, address and supervisor's name were correct. Third, I called and verified with their supervisor that they were a federal agent in good standing. This process was a way to ensure that I was dealing with a legitimate person not an individual trying to get information fraudulently. **Practice safe personal security while**

on vacation. As a Captain in the Army, I was selected to represent the United States as a North Atlantic Treaty Organization (NATO) Delegate. Because of this position, I spent quite a bit of time in Europe mostly in Brussels, Belgium. During this time, I witnessed a few examples of what not to do while away from home. One example occurred one evening when a Colonel thought it would be neat to walk three blocks from our hotel at night after he had a couple too many cocktails. Little did he know that two blocks from the hotel was the start of the famous Brussels Red Light District and traveling in this area alone at night is not advised by the local law enforcement. But the colonel either did not think anything would happen to him, or did not take the time to listen to the warnings and went. He was robbed and beaten. The next morning he looked liked he just stepped out of the ring with Mike Tyson. He learned his lesson the hard way.

While traveling with your family, always know where you are going. Either ask at your hotel or get a map and review it before you leave. Sightseeing is fun, but can be dangerous if you do not understand the environment you are entering. A trip to the Grand Canyon is very different from a trip to Bangkok, Thailand. The Grand Canyon has many elevation, steep ridges and wild animal concerns; Bangkok delivers the threat of violent crime and political unrest. Understanding the risks in planning your trip and being observant of what is going on around you while you are traveling is extremely important.

If you are caught up in the middle of an incident while traveling abroad or in the U.S., never head towards an incident or disturbance, and be careful about taking photographs. Find whatever safety you can. In the immediate aftermath, account for your family. Try to communicate by phone for help, but remember volume of cellular traffic increases during emergencies. You may have to find a regular phone to make a call. Get away from the place of incident and go to a hotel, hospital or known office location.

Once at a place of safety, continue to communicate. Even when telephone lines are down, email and broadband links sometimes stay in operation. If your attempt at communication has failed altogether, take whatever steps you can to get a message to the proper authorities. When traveling abroad, it is important to stay at the place of safety until you have notified some-one of your plans. If you see other foreigners similarly affected, stay together and pool your resources. Avoid the temptation to relocate. If you do need to relocate, check to see if your route is clear and inform someone outside of your lo-cation of your plans. Most importantly, comfort your family and tell them everything is going to be alright.

The importance of knowing information about where you are traveling is crucial. Parents must take the extra time and effort to plan their trip and ensure measures are in place if some-thing goes wrong. Vacations are meant to be fun. With a little planning and common sense, a family vacation can be relaxing, rewarding, and can make you look like the greatest parents in the eyes of your children. And isn't that what we all want?

Tips:

- Dress as inconspicuously as possible and avoid obvious displays of wealth. Don't dis-play cash, wear expensive jewelry or carry valuables such as laptop computers or cam-eras.

- Communicate to your children what they should do if they are approached by a stranger.

- Never give out personal information while you are traveling.

- Be aware of the city's geography and avoid high-crime areas (often lower-income districts) if possible.

- Avoid disputes, demonstrations, political rallies and commotions on the street. Do not stay to watch or photograph them.

- Ignore verbal comments from strangers and do not get into an argument.

- If lost, do not stand in the street consulting a map. Go to a busy shop and ask for directions or, if you must, look at the map inconspicuously.

- Always carry some form of communication equipment, such as a cellular phone programmed with numbers that would be useful in an emergency (police, embassy, etc.)

- If traveling in a foreign country that speaks a foreign language, memorize important local phrases (yes, no, how much, stop here, etc.)

- Avoid walking in city streets after dark, especially if alone. If you are walking, take only well lighted, busy streets.

- Always be alert to your surroundings. Be wary of loiterers and remember that attackers often pass their victims and then attack them from behind.

- If you suspect you are being followed, enter any busy public place and call for help.

- Adults should limit alcohol intake. You are more vulnerable to an attack if you have been drinking.

- Never accept food or drinks from strangers. Criminals often use such opportunities to drug victims.

- Use only accredited taxi services. Check to ensure the taxi drivers registration with picture is posted and matches the description of the taxi driver.

- Put your cash in more than one pocket and keep a small amount in a top pocket to hand over to a criminal who confronts you. You can also carry a dummy wallet with a small amount of cash and an expired credit card.

- If attacked, cooperate with assailants and do not make eye contact or sudden movements. Resistance is more likely to provoke violence. However, under **no** circumstances should you go with your assailant to a second location.

Chapter 16: Is The Hotel I Booked Safe For My Family?

According to a May, 2009, USA Today article, more than a billion travelers stay at U.S. hotels each year. Are hotels safe? More importantly, do you feel safe reserving, checking-in and staying at a hotel? Hotel experts are on both side of the spectrum when it comes to hotel security. Some experts say hotels are less safe following the September 11th, 2001 terrorist attacks. Others say there is no evidence that hotel crime is on the rise.

Because I believe there is no right answer and each hotel differs in security procedures, I heavily recommend that families planning to stay at a hotel continue to practice safe habits before and during their stay.

Identifying Risks:

Although hotels are required to provide reasonable care to ensure guest safety, they are not required to guarantee guest security. As a result, you should take precautions to ensure your personal security and the security of your property. Don't assume that hotels belonging to a national chain are safer than non-chain hotels as franchises don't necessarily have to follow corporate security standards. Remember, hotel guests become victims despite the sense of security locked doors, surveillance cameras and hotel staff provide.

When traveling with your family, it is important to be choosy when you pick your hotel. Your hotel room becomes your home for the night and is your sanctuary. You should thoroughly check out a hotel before making a decision. This includes avoiding properties right off interstate highways or in a problematic crime area. These are highly visible targets and easily accessible to criminals.

While conducting hotel security assessments for Corporate America, I focused on the threat of terrorism and violent crimes when analyzing each hotel. With the terror incidents in Manila, Mumbai and the past one in Jakarta, there is a constant threat regarding acts of terrorism. A family needs to take the threat of terrorism into consideration when they are shopping for hotels, but I believe their biggest risk is protecting themselves and their valuables from opportunistic criminals.

A major security issue is when analyzing a hotel is determining who has access to a guest's hotel room. While we can install electronic locks and keep a closely controlled system of key control, it is the hotel guests themselves who often let down their guard and fail to lock their door when they go out to get ice at the end of the hall or open their door to an uninvited intruder. It is important to remember that a hotel is a public place and criminals are attracted to places where outsiders are vulnerable. This can happen both day and night.

Hotel burglars are the most common type of criminal. They work mostly during the day when a room is more likely to be unoccupied. Most burglars work alone and tend to probe a hotel looking for the right room and the right opportunity. Burglars don't want to be confronted and will usually flee when approached. Most hotel burglaries do not result in violence unless the criminal is cornered and uses force to escape.

Hotel room invasion robbers, in contrast, work more often at night when rooms are more likely to be occupied and less staff is on duty. They target the occupant of a hotel room and not necessarily the hotel. A family can be targeted if the family lacks security measures and attentiveness. A robber may follow victims to their hotel room based on the value of the car they were driving or the jewelry or clothes they were wearing. Hotel room invaders usually work alone or with just one accomplice and they rely on an overwhelming physical confrontation to gain control and instill fear in the occupant.

Instill in your family members the need to practice good security techniques by locking doors, not leaving expensive items unattended in your hotel room and not telling strangers your hotel room number. It is very important for your whole family to be alert while staying at a hotel.

Tips:

Check-in precautions:

- When you arrive at the hotel room, be sure that the sliding glass doors, windows, and connecting room doors are locked.

- Never let hotel employees accompany you to your room without first checking their identity with the front desk.

- Tell the receptionist that there will be no room key duplications without your permission.

- When returning at night, use the main entrance. Don't hesitate to ask a hotel employee to accompany you to your room. Keep the door shut when you're in the room and use all the locks provided.

- If you're a woman traveling alone with a child, request a room on the second floor, as close as possible to the front desk.

- When you return to your room, check the bathrooms and closets to make sure they are empty.

- Make sure your room number has been written down, not given verbally. Because you do not want someone to overhear what hotel room your family is staying in.

What to look for in a safe hotel:

- If possible, select a hotel which has installed electronic guest room locks which are opened with a card. The majority of these locks automatically change the lock combination with every new guest so there is little chance of someone having a duplicate key to your room. If you lose or misplace your key, ask to have your room re-keyed immediately.

- Make sure each room is equipped with a deadbolt lock and a peephole.

- Each room telephone should allow outside dialing.

- Ensure that the hotel operator does not give out room numbers when receiving calls for guests. They need to transfer the call without giving the number. Also, ensure that the receptionist does not give a visitor your room number upon request.

- Secure locks on windows and adjoining doors.

- Well lighted interior hallways, parking structures and grounds.

- The parking garage should not have elevators taking passengers to guest floors. It should only go to the lobby.

- Check to see if the hotel is located in a high crime rate area, especially when traveling overseas.

Conclusion

I love this country and I love the free spirits of our children and their innocence. I love the fact that parents will do anything for their children. That is why writing this book for me was a no-brainer. I wanted to give parents a guide to help keep their children safe. I want all children to remain innocent and to feel safe. I understand that a child's safety net needs to be built and controlled by us. But as you know, we cannot be by them 24 hours a day and 365 days a year, so we need to be engaged and understand the surroundings they are in. That is our duty and our responsibility.

Trust your instincts. The world we live in is a fast-paced world with many moving parts. But as an adult and a caregiver for children, we must grasp the world around us and focus in on the security of our personal world. If something feels wrong, assume there really is something wrong.

We must provide the safest environment for our children. We must because as each parent, grandparent, uncle, aunt, and friend knows, the love for a child is endless and has no boundaries. We would do anything to keep our children safe and wish our only worries were them getting hurt on their Huffy bikes or playing football with the Mattison boys.

Securing Smiles

Useful References

Federal Bureau of Investigations:

http://www.fbi.gov/

Bureau of Alcohol and Tobacco, Firearms and Explosives:

http://www.atf.gov/

US Marshals service:

http://www.usmarshals.gov/

Bureau of Prisons:

http://www.bop.gov/

US Department of State:

http://www.state.gov/youthandeducation/

Internet Crime Complaint Center:

http://www.ic3.gov/preventiontips.aspx

Computer Crime& Intellectual Section:

http://www.cybercrime.gov/cc.html

Homeland Defense:

http://www.dhs.gov/xprepresp/

Minneapolis Police Department:

http://www.ci.minneapolis.mn.us/police/

St. Paul Police Department:

http://www.stpaul.gov/index.aspx?nid=3048

McGruff, National Crime Prevention Council:

http://www.mcgruff.org/

Crimes Against Children Resource Center:

http://www.unh.edu/ccrc/

Phoenix Police Department:

http://www.phoenix.gov/Police/

Department of Education:

http://www.ed.gov/index.jhtml

On Guard Online:

http://www.onguardonline.gov/#

Ready.Gov:

http://www.ready.gov/

Federal Trade Commission:

http://www.ftc.gov/

USA Jobs:

http://www.usajobs.gov/securityTips.asp

GetNetWise:

http://kids.getnetwise.org/tools/

The National/State Sex Offender Website:

http://www.fbi.gov/hq/cid/cac/registry.htm

Securing Smiles

Securing Smiles

Securing Smiles